Keep *and give away*

Keep and give away

Susan Meyers

Foreword by Terrance Hayes

To Michael,
With fond memories and
gratitude for the Queens
MFA experience —

Best always,
Susan
May 2006

THE UNIVERSITY OF SOUTH CAROLINA PRESS

*Published in Cooperation with the South Carolina Poetry Initiative,
University of South Carolina*

© 2006 University of South Carolina

Published by the University of South Carolina Press
Columbia, South Carolina 29208

www.sc.edu/uscpress

Manufactured in the United States of America

15 14 13 12 11 10   09 08 07 06   10 9 8 7 6 5 4 3 2 1

Library of Congress Cataloging-in-Publication Data

Meyers, Susan, 1945–
    Keep and give away / Susan Meyers; foreword by Terrance Hayes.
        p. cm.
    "Published in cooperation with the South Carolina Poetry Initiative,
    University of South Carolina."
    ISBN-13: 978-1-57003-670-5 (pbk : alk. paper)
    ISBN-10: 1-57003-670-5 (pbk : alk. paper)
    I. Title.
    PS3613.E9855K44 2006
    811'.54—dc22   2006008590

The South Carolina Poetry Book Prize is an annual prize given to the winning
manuscript of a contest organized and sponsored by the South Carolina Poetry
Initiative. The winning title is published by the University of South Carolina
Press in cooperation with the South Carolina Poetry Initiative.

For Blue

In memory of Mae Irvin Laughter (1909–2000)

I, who have never made a life within myself.

—Judy Jordan, *Carolina Ghost Woods*

Contents

Need Has Nothing to Do with It

Small Bones of Contention

Foreword

In "Her Best Note," one of the early poems in this splendid book, Susan Meyers evokes Maria Callas: "her voice so rich I almost lean / too far and fall / but I'm caught." Indeed we too "almost lean too far and fall," coaxed by the music and emotion of these elegiac poems. What catches us is the apt blend of sincerity and technique this poet employs. Throughout the book there are precisely articulated moments in which the seemingly ordinary is illuminated and transformed. Consider, for example, the reposefulness in the opening lines of poems in the first section: "You sit on the front steps in love / with the little birds" (from "Contraries"); "You sit in your swing, like a loose limb" (from "Your Mother Forbids You to Leave the Yard"); "That day I was swinging in my backyard / my body a weight / wishing for wings" (from "A Good Idea"); "I skate along a green silk thread, / my eyes half closed" (from "Her Best Note"). In each case what begins in quietude or casualness is inevitably charged by Meyers's imagination. "Contraries" ends:

> Now the finches & sparrows are back
> with two chickadees, all astir,
> flitting their soft agitation.
> Once again you fall
> for the little birds, their flutter
> of *yeses* quickening the air.

Birds are a recurring image throughout the book. They come to represent, at least to my mind, the search for simultaneous movement and stillness ("soft agitation"). In "Neither the Season, Nor the Place," the book's second to last poem, "the loons / sound wounded, but they're not." Like the image of those loons diving and resurfacing later in the poem, this collection is hinged on opposing gestures. As the title suggests, this is a book balancing all we must "keep" for ourselves with all we must "give away."

Even the language of these poems manages to be both layered and open—complex but not difficult, clear but not simplistic. Familiarity, sentimentality, nostalgia: the commonplace is elevated and deepened in the skillful hands of this poet. The work is tempered by the wisdom attained, not through cleverness or discursiveness, but through patience. Not just the patience of craft (which is abundantly evident here), but the patience of mediation, of looking. Meyers manages, incredibly, to be a witness both as Emily Dickinson was a witness, watching almost invisibly as the world unfolds around her, and as Walt Whitman was a witness, willingly participating in the joy and sadness of that world. In "Someone Near Is Dying," one of the poems fueling the book's essentially elegiac mood, one sees this tension of inaction and action at work. The opening couplets begin:

> To sit for hours by your bed
> is to gaze at the day's periphery,
>
> the chickadee at the feeder fidgeting
> like a four-o'clock insomniac.
>
> My desire is to leap into the midst
> of forgetfulness, its dreamy scatter.
>
> What does your every move show
> if not, *I am still alive?*

But maybe it's too simple to say this book's mood is essentially elegiac. "I am still alive" resists the posture of elegy. As with the whole of the book, the elegy becomes a kind of ode when the speaker addresses the "someone near [who] is dying," saying in the poem's closing: "Listen, Mother— / thunder, out of season: an old woman / at the end of her day, humming." This humming echoes the sentiments of "Her Best Note," as music and imagination bolster the speaker. *Keep and Give Away* offers us countless resounding, delicate notes. We might fall, submit to loss, were there no art such as this to keep us upright in the world.

TERRANCE HAYES

Acknowledgments

Grateful acknowledgment is made to the editors of the following publications in which these poems first appeared, some in slightly different versions:

American Poetry Journal: "Hat of Many Goldfinches"
Apostrophe: "Alterations"
Asheville Poetry Review: "Koi"
Award-Winning Poems (The North Carolina Poetry Society): "Late One Friday Afternoon"
Christian Century: "October Song," "Washing the Breakfast Dishes, I Decide"
Crazyhorse: "Guitar," "Awaiting My Brother's Pathology Report, My Husband and I Take to the River"
Crucible: "An Early Spring Morning of My Mother's Decline," "Small Bones of Contention," "Something Green, for My Mother," "Sorry," "What the Season Has Come To"
Greensboro Review: "My Mother, Her Mornings"
Icarus International: "Daughter"
Pembroke: "A Good Idea," "Weather"
Point: "Selling My Mother's House"
Southern Poetry Review: "Someone Near Is Dying"
Southern Review: "Breath," "Keep and Give Away," "Neither the Season, Nor the Place," "That Year," "Villanelle for Gertrude Stein"
Tar River Poetry: "Contraries," "Counting on the Slightest Chance," "Cradle and All," "Mother, Washing Dishes,"

"The One Place," "Primary Lessons," "Shelling: Ars Poetica," "Trying to Get It Right," "The Wheelbarrower," "Your Mother Forbids You to Leave the Yard"

"The Catch," "Her Best Note," "My Mother, Her Mornings," and "Selling My Mother's House" appeared in the chapbook *Lessons in Leaving,* winner of the Seventh Persephone Press Book Award, judged by Brendan Galvin. "Primary Lessons" appeared on Poetry Daily (www.poems.com). "Contraries," "Keep and Give Away," and "Neither the Season, Nor the Place" appeared on Verse Daily (www.versedaily.org). "Koi," "Neither the Season, Nor the Place," and "The Wheelbarrower" were published in *A Millennial Sampler of South Carolina Poetry* (Ninety-Six Press). "Fishing the Edisto" received an International Merit Award from *Atlanta Review.*

Several poems received awards from the South Carolina Academy of Authors, the North Carolina Poetry Society, *Crucible,* and the Sumter County (S.C.) Cultural Commission. My gratitude to these organizations and publications for their recognition and support.

I thank Terrance Hayes for selecting this manuscript and the University of South Carolina Press and all those who took part in awarding the SC Poetry Book Prize. I wish to acknowledge specifically the Queens University of Charlotte M.F.A. program in creative writing and the South Carolina Poetry Initiative—especially Cathy Smith Bowers, who helped shape the manuscript, and Ron Rash, Alan Michael Parker, and Kwame Dawes for their careful reading and insightful suggestions. Ed Madden and the First-Book Project also offered invaluable feedback, as did Barbara Presnell, Tom Lombardo, and many other valued poet friends too numerous to name. A huge debt of gratitude is owed to my early mentors Judy Goldman and the late Paul Rice for years of instruction and guidance. And, always, my deepest gratitude goes to my husband, Blue.

Trying to get it right

Contraries

You sit on the front steps in love
with the little birds, the finches
& sparrows fidgeting from leafy cover,
not that they need you
cheering them on to eat the seed
at the feeders hung just for them—
sunflower, millet, a white sock of thistle;
but when the hawk lowers its broad
red shoulders and sits, alone,
on the limb of the cherry tree,
after the little birds, seeing it coming,
have scattered like *ifs* and *when*s

you pull for the hawk, admiring
its heft, the turn of its head,
not to mention the unblenched eyes,
its black-banded tail. How could you not
root for this brown serenity lifting off,
grudgeless and oblivious to grudge?
Now the finches & sparrows are back
with two chickadees, all astir,
flitting their soft agitation.
Once again you fall
for the little birds, their flutter
of *yeses* quickening the air.

Your Mother Forbids You to Leave the Yard

You sit in your swing, like a loose limb
dangling from the biggest branch
which knows trunk, which knows ground.

You pump and stretch, kicking up
speed on this furious horse
until you soar past your neighbor's garage.

Below you the dog wags his tail. Inside,
the old clock travels the day,
its pendulum sweeping hill valley hill.

Whoosh is the song in your ear, wind
then mutinous hair in your face.
Comes the wind again, forgiving

as a mother watching at the window,
her arms folded, wishing
away love's daily punishments.

The morning moon wears lace, white
as your grandmother's hair.
You laugh and touch it with your toe.

Lean back into the rhapsody of air.
Lost child, close your eyes.
Let the wide sky lap you up, and up.

That Year

for my mother

When the black-eyed susans begin to bloom
in the backyard, and the moonbeam coreopsis
bursts into tiny stars, I think of the year

I banished yellow from my life. It was the year
I dug up the lantana, when I didn't plant
narcissus and all the buttery bulbs

but chose white, and a little blue, for the garden
without knowing that I was readying
for two long years of her dying. The next spring

I painted our kitchen, once a lemony gloss, ecru.
I threw out from my closet all the blouses
hinting, from their hangers, of glad canaries.

Beginning that fall I dressed in a dull haze
of beige, toning myself down for the end.
I ignored the incandescence of morning, the amber

of dusk, and leaned to clouds billowed in black.
The week in November she died I loaded the trunk
of my car with flats of pansies, three sacks of bulbs.

I wanted my hands working the dirt, a dark loam
that would spring into jonquils, daffodils—bright
coronas of yellow, and yellow, and yellow.

Ghazal of the Past

I feared the old woman, her shoe, years ago.
What Mother Goose enchanted you years ago?

I sweep a circle, my days earmarked and caged.
When did I first land in this zoo? Years ago.

A retired tenor sings his refrain, off-key:
Act wiser than you did a few years ago.

Morning climbs in my window, panting, half-cocked.
I wake to grief I never knew years ago.

Understanding keeps to itself, when it comes—
late, like a library book due years ago.

Forget sagacity, Susan. It's not here.
Your miracle rode winds that blew years ago.

Late One Friday Afternoon

Johnny Miller and I stood at the curb,
rocking our feet on its slope,
waiting for his sister Linda.
He was five. I was nine. I held his hand
nested like a bird in my palm

and with my other hand brushed dirt
from his knee. Then the bird fluttered
and was gone. Tires screeched.
I saw pieces of a toy truck
land in the Leflers' yard.

I saw blue plaid lying in the street.
My daddy, almost never home early,
leaped from the porch and ran
to the car, where a man got out.
They picked up Johnny and drove away.

We lived near the hospital. Some days
I'd watch the red streak
of Hartsell's ambulance wail by.
That day I stood as neighbors drifted
from houses, mostly mothers and children

talking in twos and threes.
Some friends told me not to worry.

An eighth grader I didn't know well
walked up to me and asked
Why did you let go?

A Good Idea

That day I was swinging in my backyard,
my body a weight
                    wishing for wings.

I closed my eyes to the dead grass,
the wind numbing my knuckles and knees.
My feet dragged the bare spot
                    to slow me down.

Chickens scratched near the fence.

From a jacket pocket I pulled last winter's
purple gloves, one cupping the other
and warm already.
                    I climbed the monkey bars,

swung hand to hand, rung to rung—fast,
until halfway across I lost my grip
                    and fell.

I lay on my back looking up, crying
because I hurt
                    and the day was cold
and I was five and the gloves had unraveled
a good idea—maybe my first.

The chickens
kept scratching. Above me that ladder rose
to the fleecy sky, then laid itself down,
breaking its promise
                    to take me somewhere.

Primary Lessons

The bus is a box, the children
obedient as crayons.
Each morning one by one
they climb into rows, thoughts
scattered out windows,
leaning toward that time of day
when they can wander outside the lines,
mark up the evening air
with the whirl of bicycle tires,
arc of a swing.
The older ones think of sundown
when long, waxy shadows
soften every sidewalk they can imagine.
The youngest want to step on a crack,
break your mama's back.

On the way home they laugh
around corners,
stripe the street with smiles.
The first to spill out, the girl in plaid,
peels off her jacket and breaks into a run,
tennis shoes flecking the grass.
The bus fades behind her.
Under the April sky she colors her day
and everything in it:
red house, blue dog, bright yellow
song of her particular art.

Trying to Get It Right

At ten I thought popular girls had everything
to hide, at least the older ones. They spoke
a language the rest of us wanted to learn,
a vocabulary all the boys understood. If only
we could decipher what we lacked, we could correct
the bad grammar of our elbows and knees.

On the bulletin board one September I saw *adverb*
and thought the teacher would never let us in
on the secret. She didn't mention the word for days
while it sat there like a perfect body. I knew
it spelled what I needed, something gorgeous
or an action I could learn to perform, a long verb

we hadn't been ready for at six: *Don't run, Spot—*
accelerate! Not only long but more sophisticated,
and wily, than any verb we'd ever encountered.
I could see it poised at sentence end, daring
to stand alone, aloof, like Bobby Helwig
blowing smoke rings on the playground.

Later, after my world was modified, I found out
the part about blowing smoke was all I got right.
I was taught to snub adverbs, treat them like boys
so slick a girl could forget herself, not to mention
the danger of excess. I was left on my own
to learn how to flirt with them, discriminately.

Sorry

Just as I pick up my fork to take the first bite
of Greek salad at my favorite restaurant,
a song rips through the room. It's Brenda Lee
in her loudest contralto. She's sorry, so sorry,

and the whole world turns on apology.
The hostess tells the waitress, "Delores,
your first table dropped their silverware."
Such a fuss. And they're sorry, so sorry.

Here in my little booth I'm fifteen again
and in love. Too young, I know,
but it's a course I've already signed up for
and I'm a serious student. Which means I play

the same record over and over
and wear my eraser down to its metal rim
doing equations that don't quite balance.
Out my bedroom window gulls are crying

in the plowed field behind our house.
I study conjugations and the phone.
In my blue notebook I write his initials
beside mine. I write my first name with his last,

and I name our children, so it must be love.
Six months—no, eight—it'll take
to shake this thing, call it what you will.
Here comes Delores. Today's olives are smaller

than usual, one pepper instead of two. If I knew
I wouldn't be sorry, I'd order the apple pie.

Her Best Note

I skate along a green silk thread,
my eyes half closed, the day unspooled.
Maria Callas sings,
her voice so rich I almost lean
too far and fall, but I'm caught
by warm honey the hour is dipped in.
Cumulus clouds float by
as if I'd ordered them for lunch.
The sky is that deep cerulean
you could sink into, plumbless and pure.
When Maria hits her best note,
I want to touch the cool cheeks
of my seven children, call them each
by name. Benjamin, Alice, Mary Elizabeth,
Joyner, Cornelia, Lacie, Thomas.
Yet by the time I'm willing to admit
I have none, the song is gone.

Cradle and All

for Erin

For forty weeks she learned a cradlesong.
On the porch, at noon, she rocks the rain away.
She would've sung to her baby all night long.

What she knows: the careless wind is wrong
to tip the treetops, cause the bough to sway.
For forty weeks she learned a cradlesong.

She jumps—a sudden thunderbolt beyond
the pines—her rocker's still, horizon gray.
She would've sung to her baby all night long.

A neighbor's crying child across the pond
unleashes wails that words, with craft, can't say.
For forty weeks she learned a cradlesong

to hum, and wait, the way the silvered lawn
is there to catch the sun's itinerant rays.
She would've sung to her baby all night long.

A slant of needles falling, wind grown strong—
her son, in some other world today.
For forty weeks she learned a cradlesong
she would've sung to her baby all night long.

Washing the Breakfast Dishes, I Decide

. . . what noun
would you want
spoken on your skin
your whole life through?
        —Mark Doty

Wren. I considered
open-mouthed words—*love,*
honor, even *melancholy*
for the sound of it—
afraid I might waste
this chance, like the one wish.
Then I remembered last Thursday's
small brown bird on the rail,
its head tilted back
in what I imagined sudden joy,
though I know its trill,
sweet and full,
rose from the breast of instinct,
the throat of an ordinary day.

Villanelle for Gertrude Stein

Buttons, tender, and delicate as rain,
require both hands, reciprocal, with trust.
Patiently we undo and do again.

What closing argument lies free of blame?
I give you two: old clasps without rust—
buttons, tender, and delicate as rain.

We close a gap, expect an inch of gain.
We've fastened nothing, wishes more or less.
Patiently we undo and do again.

Unanswered questions, the day's refrain,
we turn over and over, like a child's first
buttons, tender, and delicate as rain.

A double-threaded shank can break, the same
as someone's word. What's loved is lost.
Patiently we undo and do again.

Love when anchored can still grow, retain
its mysteries of give and take—lustrous
buttons, tender, and delicate as rain.
Patiently we undo and do again.

Alterations

Someone made a mess of this hem,
left the edge raw, and look!
the puckered seam. Who threaded
a path so crooked? This is not sewing,
this blunder. You sit in the yard undoing—

ripping stitch by stitch, your lap heavy
with fabric, wondering what it's like
being the worst at what you do.
And the oddest mystery, color: why
on an emerald dress, this lime thread?

Were you not supposed to notice?
Easier for you to ignore the redwing
blackbird riding the tallest cattail.
Maybe other birds will line their nests
with these bright threads, reweave

what's undone. Someday this dress,
or the skirt of it, you'll cut to pieces
for a quilt. It's late. If you keep moving
your chair till it's time to fix supper,
you can stay in this patch of light.

Mother, Washing Dishes

       She rarely made us do it—
we'd clear the table instead—so my sister and I teased
that someday we'd train our children right
and not end up like her, after every meal stuck
with red knuckles, a bleached rag to wipe and wring.
The one chore she spared us: gummy plates
in water greasy and swirling with sloughed peas,
globs of egg and gravy.

       Or did she guard her place
at the window? Not wanting to give up the gloss
of the magnolia, the school traffic humming.
Sunset, finches at the feeder. First sightings
of the mail truck at the curb, just after noon,
delivering a note, a card, the least bit of news.

October Song

What is the soul?
I cannot stop asking.
        —Rumi

She stitches crows across the sky
and mends a morning of pale light.

She suns and plumps the earth's pillows,
sweeps away a dust of dull leaves,

polishing, polishing

to ready this blue room
for tomorrow's company of rain.

My Mother, Her Mornings

She gathers silver-plated knives
and lays them down beside her.
She could close her eyes
to stitch the pieces
   if she had to.
Once, for her baby girl, white
batiste drifted from a yoke
of smocked elephants.

She squats on the floor,
takes to her knees,
crawling down yards of yellow.
With a sweep of her palm,
centerfold to selvage,
she persuades away wrinkles
as if brushing off crumbs.

She weights the tissue
with the knives,
pulls pins, one by one,
from her mouth,
rocks them all the way through.
Where two black dots are stamped
she dreams a pocket,
a thin shadow of gathers
to hold a daughter's hand.

She sets her jaw.
The time has come to cut
what is from what isn't,
to risk not knowing
the difference.
Her best scissors lean
into curves, angle out
at notches. Bodice, skirt,

binding (extra for pocket trim),
all the jigsaw pieces
for her to puzzle.

She barely moves her knee
to start her Singer humming.
From the bobbin she hears
    Mother daughter, mother daughter,
    listen to your mother, daughter.
How flawlessly her own mother,
each year with one more child
pulling at her skirt,
could line up gingham edges
and run a seam straighter
than a roadside ditch.
Thick-shanked buttons, collars
twice stitched, how sturdy the hold.
For her own stitching she wants more.

Lately everything she wants
hangs basted in the air,
lingers with the smell
of dotted swiss
    as if white tufts
    tick away the hours

in well-behaved rows,
as if the weave
holds a daughter's days
long after the hem is chalked,
long after the sash is tied.

Daughter

I will fly you to the city.
Stars will light the black
sky as you land.

                    That's a lie.

             Expect more light
             than dark can hold.

You must learn to live with it
like dreams stacked in the corner.
Sleep with your eyes open.

I will send you to the mountains
where a breeze sketches your face,
daisies bleach the lower slopes,
moss tempers the north side.

Lie down and close your eyes.

If I say *yellow,* do you feel
on your lids the silk of the sun?
                    I say *red.*

Never depend on light
to render the shapes you need.

Need has nothing to do with it

An Early Spring Morning of My Mother's Decline

In an ordinary hour of fish crows
and pure blank sky, the breeze is a voice
reminding live oaks they're alive.
Pollen sleeps in the pine boughs
and I am lost in shadows,
those long, phantom poles below.

When I was four and the future roamed
another country, I saw that same
indelible sky and wanted it.
Better than kinship of clouds,
closer than the neighbor's garage, I thought.
From our big backyard I pointed up, up
and straightened my whole body
like a clothespin winging from clean sheets.
I shifted my weight onto one foot,
tipped to the skewed balance of childhood
so my fingers could touch blue.
Stretched beyond all comfort,
and slightly dizzy, I was poised
to learn anything—
like the definition of distance,
its amplitude, my sorrow.

Selling My Mother's House

This is my last night. To lie here
on a mattress on the floor
is to beg, like a child, for one more hour.
Every door is a lesson in leaving.
The house is a story told in three days
of measuring worth: keep
her silver, the whatnot,
cedar chest, homemade cradle.
Throw out old Christmas cards.
Free the den doorknob
of all those rubber bands.
Give away the sheets,
blender, and green plaid sofa.
Need has nothing to do with it.

The house is an argument
of echoes and silence. A missing
mantel clock articulates the years.
I brush my teeth to the sound
of a waterfall, wipe my mouth
on an old washcloth, what's left
of her linens.

I know why children put off sleep,
ask for juice before bed.
On their bedroom wall just above
where the nightstand used to be,
a dark spot framed in faith.
How she got up one August night
and sprayed a larger and larger circle
to save him from a mosquito
droning its song between them
and the peace of sleep.
How he ducked under cover.
How this accidental art,
what was once mist,
barely there, and far from beauty,
is the only sign left.

Her Porch, Her Yard

Fewer blooms, though they seem larger, this season.
Look! she used to say, when some ordinary
flower—spider lily, petunia, daisy—
                             caught her attention.

She preferred a mingling of green to pruning:
peonies with roses, plumbago, fountain
grasses, blossoms tumbling in twined abandon,
                             her kind of order.

Yard or porch, she mastered them both. When porches
mattered more for sitting, hers charmed the neighbors
who looked forward to finding her out there, aproned,
                             talking the sun down.

When my mother shook her mop across the railing,
wrens, especially, liked the dusty shower:
strings and lint suspended in air, those tiny
                             promises of nests.

October, What the Mountains Say

They stutter their colors across the sky,
green turning yellow turning red,
each leaf a word before it dies.

Better to say than to have said,
where sassafras leaves converse all fall,
green turning yellow turning red.

A summer tanager flits, forestalls
departing—the familiar now ablaze—
where sassafras leaves converse all fall.

Crows debate how many days
till snow, when mountains are fast
departing the familiar. Now ablaze,

bittersweet, possumhaw, oak at last
unburden themselves, let loose their chatter
till snow. When mountains are fast

renouncing their mute summer manner,
they stutter their colors across the sky.
Unburden themselves, let loose their chatter,
each leaf a word before it dies.

Still Water

More than marginal,
a gloss its striders depend on.

Prefaced by duckweed. Argument
with the merely clever,
philosophy of sunrise and lily.

Marked by the day's drift of pollen,
turning page of a sky
that keeps two secrets: daylight

and night—all this, fully indexed,
leaf by floating leaf.

Something Green, for My Mother

Until I was eleven, we lived in the hills:
red clay and oak leaves big enough to kick around
in October. Then we moved east to open fields
and water oaks with their slender little leaves,

land of my father's people. My mother
missed her hills. The first fall she laughed
to see the rake sift through the leaf slivers.
She thought all that raking of little brown ovals

was for nothing. Still, she combed our yard clean
and piled a tremble of leaves at the curb.
Whenever she worked her rake or broom
or mop, she left a shine. Last year

the day after Thanksgiving she gave her old
brooms to my brother and sister and me.
For months I put mine away, not wanting it
to fall apart. This morning I took it out,

swept the porch and steps. I want to wash
the windows, mop the kitchen floor.
Tomorrow, paint something green—
our front gate—make it glisten to a shine.

Weather

The wind is up, stirring sky and sea,
hiding the horizon
    and something dreaded,
I don't know what.
        Through all this fog
who can predict the course of a storm?

My mother has been up since dawn, tentative
in her travel from bed to dresser to closet,
each step
    a necessary thought.
Her hands wade through the weight of air
hunting for pills to ward off danger. Stroke
of bad luck,
    how the body abandons
light and ease. On her slow days

she used to grate a coconut down to nubs,
mop the kitchen floor, wash and string
a week's clean living on the line.
Hanging out clothes
    was her small miracle.
She'd slide the little bag down the wire,
plucking pins
    and snapping out wrinkles
until she'd lined up sheets, towels,

every colorful stitch,
                as if we ourselves
danced there, bright
        and neat in the wind.

And now the wind has bullied the sky
into black-bottomed clouds,
                the horizon
a pale, thin lip on the sea,
        reconciled to hard and certain rain.

Someone Near Is Dying

To sit for hours by your bed
is to gaze at the day's periphery,

the chickadee at the feeder fidgeting
like a four-o'clock insomniac.

My desire is to leap into the midst
of forgetfulness, its dreamy scatter.

What does your every move show
if not, *I am still alive?*

If this moment, bare as twigs,
is the only one, let it be

the limb, in its loose skin
of lichen, tilting at clouds—

not the branch stunted
from lack of promise or light.

The beauty of Spanish moss is the curl
of its beard lifted by wind; of brown

grass, its inclination toward green;
of the chickadee, its brave opinion

of strangers. Listen, Mother—
thunder, out of season: an old woman

at the end of her day, humming.

Prayer

Send me a cleansing storm, clouds
dipping near my shoulders.

Loose, pentecostal clouds. Old
as my dead aunts and grandmother

on my father's side. Hermit clouds,
impatient clouds. With short

tempers and long influences.
Clouds the cardinals ignore.

Swift clouds, stationary clouds,
indecisives that could go either way.

A bank of propitious clouds.
Cold, sweet rain. Windblown

goldenrods outgrassing the tallest
grasses. And doves so subtly gray

you think a patch of dirt is moving.

Cavities

1.

The mouth opens to a promise,
and the repetitive day begins.
Not the story about the train
entering the station or the plane

finding the hangar—child's play—
but the one about the little performer,
its reckless spoons of habit and deed.
Not asparagus, but breath and words

though rarely the ones we mean.
The mouth consumes; it spits out facts
and phlegm. With what noise! Poor mouth,
never coming close to perfect unless

it's married to a throat that can sing. Poor
mouth, shaper of syllables that must suffice:
   green, ineluctable, knot,
   sustenance, cave, seed.

More than breath and words, little sobs
and laughs and yawns that almost tell
the story. More than these, *yes*
and *no,* open and close. Give and take.

2.

I've been looking in the mouth of old age,
examining her teeth, straight
                    but tartared.
      Ordinary stains, you may think,
but what about the worn edges?—the rows
                    short and stubby.

      Her head rolls back
on the pillow, the bed cranked just so,
and her mouth opens wide—*Open wide,*
            wider now—its roof a thin,
pale wound. Rickety picket fence, tree stumps.
Winter weeds have found the crevices. Sour
      breath leaked from an old, old

                  morning. This was my mother,
now I am hers, wiping spittle from corners,
      leaning close to peer past all decay.
Whenever I ask her, like a friendly dentist,
she obeys the same way she taught me
            and holds still, cow-eyed
and gaping, as if caught by surprise,
long after I've brushed away all that I can
and seen more than I want to see.

Emergency Room

　　　　　　Stupid, I stand
by the table where Mother lies curled
like a comma penciled in,
　　　　　　small but clarifying,
her slacks first down to her ankles
then a heap on the floor.

　　　　　　From her, stench
and clots, dark ropes of blood—*her guts
are falling out,* this is what I think.
　　　　　　Somebody please.
Her glasses have slipped below the dents
on her nose　　*my mother*
　　　　　　not my mother.

　　　　　　I sit down, stand back up.
Buttons, three five six, the top one loose,
and two at the cuffs.
　　　　　　How she loves
this blouse—pink, no, dusty rose.
She, I, someone is calling. The nurse
says to push, tilt her left hip,
　　　　　　and this too I think:
she will die if I touch her,
　　　　　　if I don't.

Fifty-four Days

That first morning I found her lying—
god I wish I could erase this one—
in a pool of diarrhea unwashed undressed
no glasses no hearing aid almost lunchtime
she looked so small my head was a racket
of thunder it took me three times crying
to the social worker—and my face doesn't
flood readily—to get the director's attention

she couldn't talk on a good day
when they cranked her up she could
touch her nose on a good day on a good day
when I sang to her she could mouth a few words
of *row row row your boat* hers had sprung a leak
hit the rocks merrily merrily and what was I
to do some mornings I'd find her pillow-propped

in her wheelchair at the table staring
at the food she wouldn't eat
and the woman across from her begging
whoever would listen *please darlin'*
please take me home I'd spoon her lumps
of potatoes spoon and gently
spoon and wonder why why why
anybody would think anybody would want
to eat this stuff cold beans iced tea with no ice

weeks after she died I saw the news article—
a woman ninety-one her age another little white-haired
husk left lying in bed there yes *there* neglected
after a fall—wounded in the head
the woman dead in days I'm telling you this
because I checked them all and this worst
of places was the best

                    when we'd reach the end
of the song *gently down the stream*
I'd pray that life for her was nothing but a dream.

Breath

. . . to die is different from what
any one supposed, and luckier.

> —Walt Whitman

Early that last morning when I walked
into her room and saw her face, jaundiced,
as they had told me it soon would be, I called
my sister, my brother too, and sat down
   by her bed to wait.

My sister and I held her hand, rubbed
her forehead, sang hymns to her. My husband
took his turn. You'd have thought
we were coaching a birth.
   She was all breath,

and when the breath snuffled its last,
she was a thin white thing lying there,
her mouth a little *O,* where once
there had been breath. Her mouth
   was a little *O.*

Now the three of us exhaled,
   our mouths larger *O*'s

gusting out the long sobs and orphan
cries, out of each mouth's large *O,*
the room a rush of mingled breath.

When they called us back in, after
the nurse had washed her and changed her
into a clean pink nightgown,
    all was a hush,
though I wondered to myself,

gazing at her hair, wispy and white,
how she could look, already,
    like the clear, bright air
once the wind has died down—
her skin transparent, her eyes

closed now, her mouth still open
as if circling a secret.
We understood nothing, nothing,
but for weeks every word I heard
    mouthed her little *O.*

Sweetgum in January

So this is winter's toll,
spread across the map
of sky:
        all the lovely
roads are deadends

without astonishments
we hoped they'd bring.

Trafficked or bare,
        these bold
determinations limb
the uncertain air

in shapes we know
too well: bonescape
pearled in light.

Line after line
of scrawl, a script
no one can read.

Little birds flock
to crooks and turns,
each tilt

        or bob a shrug
against the cold.
Blink of come and go.

And now the cardinals,
one high,
        one low,
bright as the earth's
last two berries.

What the Season Has Come To

Winter is a bladed silver day, stripped
to its armaments. A chamber of stringed instruments.
Carded cotton, strands of darkest silk.
Not the voice but the echo, not the bride
but her reflection, not the funeral but the wake.

We want to ignore the cold, so let us break bread
with color. Red, orange, and blue bask
in the retreat of green—trees and birds lit by these,
not the open light of yellow. Winter reds surprise us,
for we know others, scarlets leafy

and reckless as autumn. The swamp waiting for spring
is a story of shimmer and light. Geography of trees.
Meditation of moss, the woods a solitary prayer.
Let us praise the verticals of winter—awakenings
of gray, rising past the sad chill of November.

For this is what the season has come to:
egret, heron, the damp smell of dirt
when all but the wind seems deciduous and still.
To shun the specter of death, winter wears a warp
of stunted days, a thin mantle of light.

Hat of Many Goldfinches

Say you could wear twenty goldfinches on your head,
ten females in their soft, modest plumage
and ten bright males.
                        What jubilation,
all that twittering and hopping about.
Little feet massaging your scalp, little beaks
perchicoreeing to everyone you pass.
                                No need for ribbons
or veils on your black and yellow nest
of excitement, your curious crown of animation.

But how to seduce the finches to stay. A sprinkle
of thistle in your hair might hold them
long enough for you to kneel
                        at the altar of morning.
Gives you goose bumps
to feel the beaks tapping against your skin.
Walking down noon's aisle, you nod
and they shift a little.
                        More shuffling,
and the hat is rearranged. Take your photo,
or look in the mirror, and the hat you see there
is another, not the same hat you wear now.

Never depend on a hat of goldfinches
                        to bore you.

And forget the hatbox. These hats rest in sweetgums
and maples, on a narrow shelving of limbs.

I once knew a woman who wore her robin hat
when the finches wouldn't come. But the hat was heavy
and the brown depressed her.
                              She stayed home that morning,
her hair crawling with worms. The day she wore her
bluebird hat the bugs bothered her breathing,
the smallest attracted to the wind of her nostrils.

                        Now she knows to wait
for the finches. As long as there are finches
there's a dream of a hat of finches—
                              the hat
we all want to wear on the day we die.
Imagine your own last dimming, its perfect
orchestration: final breath, pause,
                        a sudden fluttering
and lifting of forty somber wings.

Small bones of contention

A Counting

Two crows—no, three—plus their giant
shadows, swoop through the pines.
I tell you, the shadows count for something.

Why all this swirling of black capes,
fast, toward me? Fling nothing
across my shoulders, you glossy bad omens.

Six cronies (or is it three?) in the yard,
a covenant of crows. They know something.
One wanders so close I shudder. The others

swagger about and suddenly the warm afternoon
is an argument of seven crooks at the feeder.
One, on the feeder's roof, glints my way

then tilts his big head upside down
to reach the seed on the tray beneath his big feet.
Another, vying for Top Crow, lands beside him

and the feeder sways on its little pole.
Hold it—this is a heist, they seem to say
before they lose their balance and flee.

Five, then four, pick over the plenty
like dumb thieves left at the scene, greedy
for the loot—old seed, bare ground, hulls.

Morning Song

The rooster I do not have blinks
and struts his glossy history in the pen
I want to build beside the garage.
"No," my husband says, "pens
belong *behind* garages."

I want to watch my rooster pick
through the day's minutiae, my neighbors
listening for his early call, dreading it
the way I tolerate, late afternoons,
the baying of their deerhounds.

Every day he ruffles feathers.
Three young hens in the chicken yard
(and the brown leghorn I'll buy at the fair)
admire his hot temper and fleshy comb.
They fuss over the right to ignore him.

I love roosters, the way I love
sonatas and the Song of Solomon.
The love I'd feel for this rooster
can't live up to his diligent crowing
nor the curve of his spurs, his perfect feet.

Guitar

On any given night it picks its way
down the canyon, one step
almost in front of the other—agile enough
to slip by whatever spells trouble.
Forget fear. It slides down rocks, if it has to,
to reach bottom. By day, a red bandana
or straw hat, and why not?
No map, just crosshatch and parallel.
It inhales the heat, and the pinched cold
creeping off the mountain.
It lives alone, turns its back to the wolves.

Say it's a tin cup with bent handle.
Peyote in full bloom. A train
pulling rich cargo across the horizon.
Tequila. A thumbnail piercing the skin
of a lime, the ripe shower that follows.

The One Place

Most Sundays we don't attend, never did
except the fall my father died, and went then
because we had just moved to Minnesota—

new job, relocation—and feeling lost,
Blue and I turned to what we'd each known
as children when once a week we'd suffered

the hard pew, listening and praying,
mostly squirming, as we waited for something
to take hold. But year after year

when we go fishing, most often in spring,
boat trailer in tow, and get ahead of ourselves
with anticipation of the largemouths

waiting in the lily pads and miss
the narrow lake road to the right, its sign
hidden by an overgrowth of myrtles,

especially when it's early and still dark,
that's when we look for the steeple
and empty parking lot. The one place open

without a locked gate, without a guard
dog or chain or *No Trespassing,*
the one place allowing us—

before we've gone too many miles
in the wrong direction—to enter
its wide, forgiving drive and turn around.

The Catch

Salt in my mouth, the chalk
of the weight between my teeth.
The tide leaves the creek.
   I coil, uncoil

to cast the net.
Timing is all.
   I know this
but can do nothing to get it right.

My husband knows the balance
   of circles,
the trust he puts in the center.
Carefulness is not his
yet I see the arc
of his right hand, palm up
to twirl the net.
You're trying too hard, he says,
and it occurs to me
that's where the lines tangle.

I watch his dance.
In his left hand a veil,
folded over, as if once again
he gives her away,
the youngest, light so fond
of her hair she shimmers.
   This time it is himself
   he has come to let go.

Key West Elegy

The January breeze elates the palm
beside the bay. Anhingas, caped and calm
as old morticians, test the morning air.
Not death, but fishing, fits the bill. What balm,

what fake flamingo mercy, drew me here where
doors are turquoise—daily forecasts fair?
Roosters roam the town. The mangrove strings
its roots above the water, poised to snare

me in a tangled dream. Here the wings
of ibis scroll across the sky, their wintering
a pale calligraphy. For me, the cost
of drifting this far south? Ease that sings

with no desire to end the song. I've tossed
to sea my thoughts of heading north—frost
and leafless trees. I'll turn instead to psalm
of sunsets. Twilight, lose me, keep me lost.

Shelling: Ars Poetica

It's simple. Go where the shells are: high
tideline above the collapse of jellyfish,
below the dunes, below the stubbled
nut grass, along swash lines and rills.

There must be habit and form, sensible
as your old shirt with deep, pleated pockets.
Nudge the charred log, lucent coils
of egg casings, plastic bags weighted

and fluttering, any wash-up stubborn enough
to yield nothing till toed aside.
Learn to bend and reach, gladly,
the way a Zen master would teach you

if you had a Zen master. On a good day
you'll forget the bad news you swore
you couldn't. Humming helps, any song,
in any key. Don't expect to be squared

with the earth. Go slack-jawed, head tilted
as if nodding to a face that greets someone else;
otherwise, you'll miss the shape and shine
you're after. Find the first one fast—hold it

like a charm—and more will come.
Rub the smoothest part, inside so slick
wet and dry feel the same. Be selective—
these are not your cousins asking favors—

yet who can leave to tide an angel wing,
the scallop with one ear? Apologize
to the ones you step on. Mostly go alone
or walk behind, expecting less: followers

learn to look for the overlooked. To find
symmetry in the broken, take a child.
Stay past sundown for a pink-fevered sky.
Keep looking east. Birds will feed on fishes,

loose stitches riding the ruffled sea.
A dragonfly will sip the air. Cockles
and razor clams are yours for the stooping,
a moon snail worth the sand stinging

your eyes. If you find one, don't ask for two
but never turn down luck. It comes to this:
no matter how many, how flawless, how rare,
the last one leaves you wanting more.

Fisher's Luck

All he wants is one fish,
one largemouth he's set his mind to.
I've settled in the back of the boat with a book.

We drift into the cypress slough,
water-lilied favorite of the lone ibis
balancing, like an agile gymnast, on a limb.

Under shade it teeters, bouncing the limb,
trying to hold still, as if hidden
like the black tips of its folded wings.

I've closed my book and look
from blossom to floating white blossom,
mostly open, unfolded and fingering air,

the centers bursting with yellow.
I've never seen so many.
Here we are, a perfect pair:

one runs the trolling motor,
casts in the likely spots,
and watches the shallows for stumps

while the other sits, and sits, basking in luck.

Fishing the Edisto

1. The river

It's the wry, wrinkled face
        of a southwest breeze,

        old uncle busy
with the commerce
of leaves, drift of fuzz & reeds—

a current Blue and I follow. Drifting
heeds its own philosophy.

It's April, when birdsong
is the compass that keeps us
from losing ourselves to the sea.

 Easy to forget, so I am naming
        all the reasons we came,
the up & down, slick & shag of it.

2. Rootless & rooted

They climb and dangle: smilax,
a confidence of tangled honeysuckle.

Spanish moss lives on a dare.

The trees on both sides
stand thick-kneed
             and allegiant—cypress,
river birch, sycamore—some so tenacious,
so banked in the day, they lean out
             over water, then up.

3. Airborne

Vultures and egrets skate across the sky,
cruising to the drone of a plane, to the sweet

harmonics of other birds: cardinal, osprey—
             those are the easy ones—
warblers I need a book to identify.

             A white-throated sparrow,
its cheerless call, points me to some vague
sorrow, was it upstream or down?

What's so urgent the wren
must repeat itself, so irritating
a fish crow must mutter the last word?

4. Fish

We know the tug of them, their
            nimble dodge—and their stink.

The morning's glint & gamble,
here they're not jumping
            to any conclusions.

I net a dead shad, eyeless and limp,
just to look it over, shying away
            from the wasp
that bums a ride on the boat rail.

Blue reels in a striped bass
            too small.
When he throws it back, I fall headlong
for the unexpected song of fish
            splashing water.

Awaiting My Brother's Pathology Report, My Husband and I Take to the River

for Gene

Laughing gulls laugh, and laugh, what they do best.
Hilarious, I guess, the afternoon sun.
They can barely contain themselves. A pageant
of cedar, Chinese tallow, more cedar.
          I'm half sick
of all this beauty. Grapevines thread
the bank's bramble. An osprey repeats its pitiful call—
odd, its small cry.

     Blue stands at the bow
and whips his line past a bumblebee droning
from rod to unused rod propped up against the seat.
Fish crows talk their low crow talk.
        The bee buzzes
so near my head (almost touching my nape) I cringe
and break out in goose bumps.

      Here's the hope:
a dried-up vine clings to whatever it can.
Still there, a wrecked boat and motor,
half submerged, left to rust. A stand of sumac,
that determined weed.

Dead stumps dot the water.
We have come here to ease through something green
and growing.

Is that a bullfrog, or alligator,
bellowing low? Out here the birds are kind
with their remarks, pickerelweed thrives
in clumps.
Full to crested over, what does the river care?
A frog jumps from the bank in its long, perfect arc.
Blue switches bait. Above us a grackle
fusses and flits from limb to limb.

Koi

The smallest are pond bred, slip stitches
of the bright selves they're turning into.

The larger ones quicken the hour, shimmering
along the deepest channel and settling for constant

change. Today the pickerelweed blooms three more
purple spikes, the lizard's tail leans farther from its pot.

The fish with black-tipped fins and two white streaks
on its head swims straight down the middle, then

without pause, turns from the cool pleats
of the waterfall and swims back, as if to unravel

a mistake. The others thread in and out of rushes
and spatterdock, near the dragonfly that scissors

on the iris above. They know the shady spots
and the one that brings a late-afternoon shower

of food, as in the pearled light they gather and rise
above trees and sky to knot the day's loose ends.

Out in the Cold with the Crows

Plank by plank, Blue is rebuilding the bridge
over the fish pond. He sits on the arch,
measuring—one leg spraddled, the other
resting like a bent nail.
Sometimes I wish he were a carpenter.
Today he is. All afternoon we've stayed in touch
by walkie-talkie. If he's busy sawing—dirty
hands, muddy shoes—and wants a beer, he calls.
I respond, my only help.
The new bridge barely slopes like the belly
of a spoon turned upside down.
Once it was so steep you had to clutch
the railing to keep from sliding backward.
This time he braced it with a board underneath,
a rib down the middle. All the edges, even.
Next he plans to redo the stone walkway out front—
too low, cracked mortar.
Every rain we have to wade to the door.

It's not that he's unhandy, he's skilled,
but around here we often do things twice:
once without thinking, a second time to get it right.
The winter my mother died
he built a fence around the woods,
three rails and chicken wire at the bottom.
Too many deer and stray dogs, he said.

Day after day, for six weeks he worked
out in the cold with the crows.
He tied a string for a sightline, dug up stumps
and roots, measured and checked,
eyed it again and again
before hammering the first nail into sturdy
one-by-fours and posts set in concrete.
Yesterday was his birthday,
tomorrow would have been hers.

Counting on the Slightest Chance

The native grasses didn't wilt or grow.
They stood there, lackadaisical in sun
unwavering as Monday's rumination,
when preachers tallied numbers, fallen low,
when farmers planned their week, to plow and sow
or not, if rain, the savior, didn't come.
Like soldiers in the field, they held their ground—
the bluestems, wiregrass, sedges, inland oats.

On days in June you thought it'd never rain
it didn't. On days you knew it would, it wouldn't.
The stamina of grasses left no doubt
that hope is for the stubborn. Weather vanes
directed hope to east, to west, but couldn't
change the forecast—dry, drier, drought.

Small Bones of Contention

Tonight's the full moon, or close. Blue
and I could go walking to look for animals.
Our little woods out front turn black at night

no matter how high the moon. It's so dark, bears
could roam out there and we'd miss seeing
their oily fur rub against the loblollies.

There could be barred owls and the rabbit
that built a den near the old fence line.
I mentioned the bears as a ruse, but bats I'm sure of—

they leave their droppings on the porch railing
and splats of blood on the floor after a good night.
Blue and I close our eyes to separate dreams

of the woods. To me a tangle of vines
and enough trees—from saplings to old stumps—
to get lost in. To him a polite congregation

of the tallest trees. He likes to hear his chainsaw.
I prefer birdsong. That's not fair to say,
he likes song, too. He says he's giving more light

to the hardwoods. And I know light
is a tree's first love. What is a bear's?
Berries? The perfect eye of a full moon?

How the Living Worry

My chickens are dead. Their missing heads are whispers,
their feet upturned and feathers luckless as ashes.
The bloody pen. A weasel stole the night.

What to dwell on—chickens, weasels, or night?
Time and time again, nothing but whispers.
Sunrise more smoke than fire and ashes.

There's death in the air, a waltz of chickens and ashes.
Hard to trap that weasel stalking the night
and turning the sky, its litany of stars, to whispers.

Death is a whisper, a rain of ashes falling all night.

Our Manifold Sins

We acknowledge and bewail our manifold sins
and wickedness, which we from time to time
most grievously have committed. . . .

——from the Sacrament of the Lord's Supper

He has yelled at me, I have yelled at him
words which we from time to time most grievously
have regretted. Profane. Not killing but cruel, flung in a tone

which we from time to time most grievously have practiced
and mastered. I say *how dare you,* he says *I'm sick of,*
clichés which we from time to time most grievously have
   swapped

and embellished upon. Lodged in our throats is the wafer
of apology which we from time to time most grievously have
   swallowed
all too quickly, leaving our tongues wagging without grace

which we from time to time most grievously have failed
   to seek.
Instead we huff and shake our heads
which we from time to time most grievously have bowed

to an altar of anger. Meanwhile the morning sunlight
climbs the perfect squares of our kitchen window
which we from time to time most grievously have turned
    our backs to.

Love Poem Gone Astray

He has flown again to Florida. Come Friday
I know he'll be back, but today what I long for
is his clutter. So I'll drape his brown belt
over the closet doorknob, wad up a handkerchief

and wedge it behind the seat of his recliner.
Just when I'm trying to figure out why he loves
the broken-back Rebel on page thirty
of his fishing magazine and why he keeps a stash

of used golf tees in the Kleenex box on the vanity,
the dog in the yard behind ours starts barking
its facile complaints. And now I miss my old dog.
The first year Blue and I were married,

living in a trailer on the farm, he found me
a beagle from the want ads—Lucille
who came the moment I called. Frankly
she adored me. She would run a fifty-yard dash

through the squash and never crush a leaf,
keeping her head low, sleek as a sports car.
I should have named her Avanti. Corvette.
She was that fast. The next year when we moved

to the city, I had to give her away, a real twist
now that I think about it, my leaving Lucille,
since in the country song I named her for
the husband got dumped with children

and crops to tend, claiming she picked
a fine time to leave him. No *Come Friday*
for him. When I woke up in the hospital
after surgery—blocked tubes, no babies—

Blue was sitting by the bed, holding
my hand and talking, fast, about another beagle.
He would have promised anything.
I always told myself Lucille was happy:

squirrels to chase, creek by the woods, empty
bean field out back, that little gravel-kicking boy
hanging around the barn. Who was I kidding?
Crops or no crops, it's never easy.

Planting, the Second Year

For once he loaded the trailer with care
so now the tedious unloading. The tarp,
shining in the sun like a silver blanket,
must be untied. He bends over
as if telling the ground his best secret
and picks at the closest knot, a stubborn one.

Five more knots, each knuckled
tighter than a fist, and he'll be done.
Out of luck with this one, he tries the next.
With patience all this rope could be saved,
something his wife would praise him for.
He searches a pants pocket for his knife.

She'll have to praise his speed instead.
The tarp freed, he pulls it back slowly
as if unveiling a load of prized turkeys.
Wedged in rows, twenty yaupon hollies
lie on their sides like hoboes, weary
and cramped, napping in shiny green jackets.

He pulls them, in twos, across the grit
of the trailer's floor. Lifts them by the rim
of their black plastic pots. Sets them down
near the gravel drive, admiring them, upright

and hardy, already relaxing their stiff limbs
though still misshapen from the ride.

Seated now on the trailer's tongue
he removes his cap and swipes his sleeve
across his face, that map of sweat,
closing his eyes to conjure the dream of a man
past knots and the short shadows of noon—
rich in hollies, twenty holes to dig.

The Wheelbarrower

He winds down the gravel drive,
pushing a load of mulch,
a smaller and smaller blue shirt
threading through the pines.
I can barely see him, yet my eye
tends toward him like a stem to sun—
a study of straw hat and suspenders,
his spotted dog nosing behind. Now

he's a tiny figure in his garden.
Beyond the sweetgums south of the beans
he dumps the mulch and rakes it level.
I know the work he does. What I see
is a man bent over a handle, rocking
in rhythm, drawing it to his chest
as if saying goodbye to it one more time,
then casting it at arm's length

so he can say it over and over
until it needs no more saying.
He pulls the wheelbarrow back up the drive.
A yellow butterfly flits about his shoulders.
He keeps his head low
and passes close, his eyes cast down
as if daily work were prayer,
dirt stains on the belly of his shirt.

Neither the Season, Nor the Place

Lake Santee, S.C.

Some mornings I mutter down the hallway
of our marriage and open the only available door.
But once in a while, say on a warm January morning,
I ride out with him on the smooth lake of it,
our small boat in the midst of quivering loons,
the soprano of their notes—not calls, really,
but soft barkings—reaching out into the air
like questions that reorder the day.
In these high-pitched tones of small dogs, the loons
sound wounded, but they're not:
they drift on the honey-sweet water, unfettered
and safe in their wintering. We watch one bob
and dive, and just when we're distracted, it resurfaces
a few feet from us, a white-breasted surprise.

Another and then another loon rises in place,
stretches its thick neck, flapping its wings,
and shakes off a shiver of water. They appear
and disappear. Around us their quiet yelping, the rising
and diving—our boat rocking occasionally in another
boat's wake. Their bodies glide in a slate cloak
of understatement, not the black-and-white
plumage they're known for, their bright-checkered
beauty—this being neither the season, nor the place.

Keep and Give Away

What do I know of man's destiny?
I could tell you more about radishes.

—Samuel Beckett

With a bushel basket in hand
he's the tally of my ripest desires,

more than the sum of his summer
crops, perfect and plentiful as they are—

even counting Early Contenders
and Silver Queen. Burpless

cucumbers, Kentucky Wonders, too.
Throw in the fruit to sweeten

the numbers: blackberries and figs
piled in pyramids or weighed

in pecks. And don't forget
the peppers (red, yellow, green),

divided into *keep* and *give away.*
Dinner plates—heaped with leafiness,

tubers, and pods——heavy
with the haul and roots of his labor.

Now he's shelling peas in his lap
and I sit across the room, listening

to the ping, ping. He's more
than the sum, I cannot count the ways,

and despite a constant reckoning
of work and luck, numbers fail me

in this long, hot growing season.